P9-BBP-072

THE HISTORY OF EXPLORATION
Exploration of
SPACE

WITHDRAWN

New Forest Press

Fitchburg Public Library
5530 Lacy Road
Fitchburg, WI 53711

Publisher: Tim Cook
Editor: Guy Croton
Designer: Carol Davis
Production Controller: Ed Green
Production Manager: Suzy Kelly

ISBN: 978-1-84898-302-1
Library of Congress Control Number: 2010925462
Tracking number: nfp0003

U.S. publication © 2010 New Forest Press
Published in arrangement with Black Rabbit Books

PO Box 784, Mankato, MN 56002
www.newforestpress.com

Printed in the USA
9 8 7 6 5 4 3 2 1

All rights reserved. No part of this publication may be reproduced, copied, stored in a retrieval system,
or transmitted in any form or by any means electronic, mechanical, photocopying, recording,
or otherwise without prior written permission of the copyright owner.

Every effort has been made to trace the copyright holders, and we apologize in advance for any omissions.
We would be pleased to insert the appropriate acknowledgments in any subsequent edition of this publication.

CONTENTS

WHAT IS SPACE?   4–5

EXPLORING BY EYE   6–7

NAVIGATING THE NIGHT SKY   8–9

EXPLORING SPACE WITH
TELESCOPES   10–11

TRICKS & TECHNIQUES   12–13

ROCKETS   14–15

SPUTNIK & OTHER
SATELLITES   16–17

MOONSHOTS   18–19

ASTRONAUTS   20–21

JOURNEYS TOWARD
THE SUN   22–23

JOURNEYS AWAY FROM
THE SUN   24–25

THE SPACE SHUTTLE   26–27

TELESCOPES TODAY   28–29

THE HUBBLE SPACE
TELESCOPE   30–31

SPACE STATIONS   32–33

COSMIC PUZZLERS   34–35

MAKING CONTACT   36–37

THE FUTURE   38–39

THE BIG BANG & THE
FATE OF THE UNIVERSE   40–41

DID YOU KNOW?   42–43

GLOSSARY   44–45

FURTHER READING & WEBSITES
                                                          46

INDEX   47

ACKNOWLEDGMENTS   48

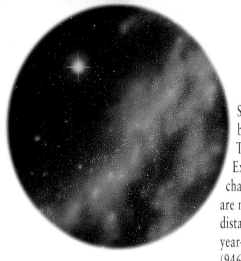

WHAT IS SPACE?

Space is the name for the part of the universe between heavenly bodies such as galaxies, stars, and planets. It is not empty. There are such things as clouds of dust and gas in space. Exploring space and all that it contains is the greatest challenge facing humankind. In space, distances are measured in light-years. This is the distance traveled by light in one year—588,000,000,000,000 mi. (946,000,000,000,000km). In thousands of years, we have only just begun to explore space. As the third millennium begins, a new generation—you—will take up the challenge.

DUSTY PATCHES

This cloudy patch is called a nebula. Some nebulae are galaxies, made up of thousands of millions of stars and many light-years away. Others are patches of dust and gas in our own galaxy, the Milky Way.

FALLING SKIES

Space is full of dust and pieces of rock. When they enter Earth's atmosphere, most of them burn up and we see meteors, or shooting stars. Sometimes a larger piece of rock reaches the surface of Earth before it burns up and hits the ground as a meteorite. For thousands of years, meteorites were the only objects from space that could be studied. This woodcut made in 1508 shows a meteorite splitting a tree in half.

CLOCKWORK MODELS

For thousands of years astronomers have been exploring the solar system, the planets, and other objects that orbit the star that we call our Sun. An orrery is a clockwork model of the solar system in which the planets orbit the Sun in the center.

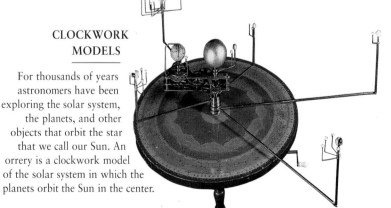

SKY WATCHING

The skies have been watched since earliest times. Observatories are buildings from which astronomers study the skies. This one, El Caracol, was built by the Maya astronomers of Chichen Itza, in what is now Mexico.

HEAVENLY BODIES

Earth is one of eight planets in the solar system. One moon orbits Earth. Our planet can be explored from space like any other heavenly body. Studying Earth as an astronomical body must be done from a satellite or spacecraft. This view of Earth has been taken far enough away to show the Moon and stars.

~c.3000 BC~
Egyptians use stars to mark the weeks in their calendar

~c.300~
Aristarchus teaches that Earth circles the Sun

~c.100~
Hipparchus compiles a catalog of stars. He constructs a model of the Sun circling the Earth: to allow for seasons Earth is slightly off-center in the circle.

~c. AD 150~
Ptolemy publishes several books on astronomy, including the Almagest. He makes a list of 1080 stars, divided into 48 constellations, and tables from which the movements of the Sun, Moon, and planets can be worked out. He teaches that the Earth is the center of the universe.

~c. 1150~
Chinese invent rockets

AN ANCIENT CALENDAR

In ancient Egypt, the year was divided into 36 weeks of ten days each. Each week started when a particular star group, called a decan, rose in the sky. This ceiling *(left)* from the temple in Dendera shows a circle supported by goddesses. Around the outside ring are figures representing the decans. In the center of the circle are the signs of the zodiac. The gods, holding wands, represent planets.

BARON MUNCHAUSEN

People have dreamed of traveling in space for centuries, although it is only in the latter half of the 1900s that they have achieved it. Baron Munchausen, the hero of an amazing collection of stories published by Rudolf Erich Raspe in 1785, disdained any form of spacecraft— he used a fast-growing bean to reach the Moon!

EXPLORING BY EYE

PTOLEMY

The earliest astronomers were not interested in how the universe worked. They needed to know when to plant or harvest crops, when rivers would flood, or when there would be an eclipse. They used the movements of bodies in the heavens to make calendars and to predict events in the future. Consequently, they became astrologers as well as astronomers. It was the ancient Greeks who first started to ask questions about the universe and how it worked. They were interested in the movements of the planets—the wandering bodies that they could see in the night sky. They wanted to prove that the movement of planets was regular and could be accurately predicted. To try to do this, they used geometry.

PTOLEMY

Ptolemy, or Claudius Ptolemaeus (A.D. 90–168) lived in Alexandria in Egypt. He was an astronomer and geographer who listed 48 constellations, or groups of stars, giving their positions in the heavens. Ptolemy argued that Earth was a sphere and believed that the Moon, Sun, planets, and stars moved around Earth at different speeds. Many of his ideas were taken from an earlier Greek astronomer, Hipparchus. Ptolemy published his ideas in a book known as *Almagest*, which translates to mean "the greatest."

TEACHING TOOLS

An armillary sphere is a 3-D diagram of the heavens. The circles stand for the celestial equator, the zodiac, and other circles in the sky. Armillary spheres were used for teaching and for taking measurements.

COPERNICUS

Nicolaus Copernicus (1473–1543) is the father of modern astronomy. From his studies, he saw that some of Ptolemy's ideas did not work. Ptolemy implied that the Moon's size changed, but it obviously did not. In the *Almagest*, Ptolemy looked at each planet separately, and it was clear that they were in some way connected. Aristarchus (c. 310–230 B.C.) thought that Earth and the other planets revolved around the Sun. Copernicus thought that this was the simplest and most systematic reason for the movement of heavenly bodies. He could not prove this Sun-centered (heliocentric) theory, but it made much more sense than the Earth-centered (geocentric) explanations.

CENTER OF THE UNIVERSE?

Early astronomers thought that Earth was the center of the heavens. They believed that Earth was fixed, and that the Sun, Moon, and planets circled around it. They thought that each planet (the Sun and Moon counted as planets) was carried by a transparent sphere of crystal that moved. Above and beyond the planets was a sphere to which the stars were attached. This diagram *(left)* shows this geocentric system.

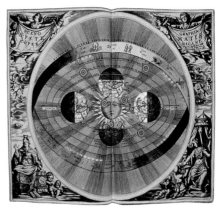

SUN-CENTERED

This diagram *(right)* shows Copernicus's heliocentric theory of the universe. The Sun is at the center, with the known planets revolving in circles around it. Copernicus published his ideas in a book called *De Revolutionibus Orbium Coelestium* just before he died in 1543.

SET IN STONE

Around 1000 B.C. the people of Mesopotamia were very interested in the heavens. This boundary stone shows the Sun, the Moon, Venus, and zodiac signs. The zodiac is the group of 12 constellations that the Sun and the planets seem to travel past during the year. They were thought to be important in predicting the future.

NEW MOONS

Muslim astronomers were particularly interested in the Moon. The Muslim month starts when the new Moon is first seen, so it was extremely important to know when this was going to happen. Muslims pray at least five times per day, so astronomers also needed to figure out exactly when sunset, nightfall, daybreak, noon, and afternoon were going to be. Many mosques employed astronomers as timekeepers. This picture shows astronomers in Istanbul around 1577. There are books on shelves and many instruments, including quadrants, a compass, and an armillary sphere. There is a clock on the table and a globe on the floor.

WINTER SKY

Orion, the Hunter *(marked below in red)*, is a magnificent constellation visible during late evenings in winter. The three stars in its belt can be used as a celestial signpost. Just below the belt is a shiny patch called the Orion Nebula, which is a splendid sight through binoculars or a small telescope. The Orion Nebula is in fact a stellar nursery, where stars are being born right now.

GEMINI

A slightly curving line drawn upward through Rigel and Betelgeuse will get you to Gemini, with its two bright stars Castor and Pollus, the Heavenly Twins.

AURIGA

Over Orion's head is Auriga, the Charioteer. Near the bright star Capella is a distinctive triangle of stars called the Kids.

PERSEUS

Now follow a line northeast of Orion past Taurus and you will come to Perseus. This constellation contains a double open cluster, which is a great sight through binoculars.

TAURUS

Follow the three stars of Orion's belt upward and you will come to the constellation Taurus, the Bull. Taurus contains the bright red star Aldebaran. This star appears to form part of the "v" of the Hyades, which is an open star cluster. In fact, Aldebaran is a foreground star and is not part of this distant group. Following the line from Orion's belt yet further, you will come to a close-knit bunch of stars called the Pleiades. These stars form yet another open cluster.

CANIS MINOR

A line to the west of Orion takes you to the small constellation Canis Minor, the Little Dog. The three stars Procyon (in Canis Minor), Betelgeuse (in Orion), and Sirius (in Canis Major) form the prominent Winter Triangle.

The Kids

PERSEUS

AURIGA

Pleiades

Castor

Pollux

GEMINI

TAURUS

Aldebaran

Hyades

CANIS MINOR

Procyon

Betelgeuse

ORION

Belt

ERIDANUS

Winter Triangle

Nebula

Rigel

Sirius

LEPUS

CANIS MAJOR

CANIS MAJOR

Canis Major, the Big Dog, is found by following Orion's belt downward. It contains Sirius, the brightest star in the sky.

LEPUS

Beneath Orion is an undistinguished constellation called Lepus, the Hare.

ERIDANUS

Eridanus, the River, is another faint constellation that manages to meander a sixth of the way around the sky. It lies to the right of Orion, just past Rigel.

NAVIGATING THE NIGHT SKY

On a clear, moonless night, over 2,000 stars can be seen with the naked eye. Ancient astronomers identified star patterns, called constellations. These patterns are purely a human invention and serve only to help astronomers find their way in the sky. In reality, what looks to us like a bright star might really only be a faint star fairly close by, whereas a genuinely bright star might appear dim to us because of its vast distance from Earth.

CEPHEUS

A straight line through Merak and Dubhe in the Plough and Polaris will take you to Cepheus, a dim constellation.

SPRING SKY

When you look up at the late evening sky in spring, you should be able to see the seven stars of the Plough. Use the Plough to navigate your way around the sky.

CASSIOPEIA

A line from Mizar in the Plough through Polaris takes you to the constellation Cassiopeia, a beautiful w-shaped constellation through which parts of the Milky Way pass.

DRACO

Between Ursa Major and Ursa Minor is long, winding Draco, the Dragon, a fairly dim constellation.

URSA MINOR

Follow the two stars Merak and Dubhe in the Plough northward and you will come to Polaris, the Pole Star, in the constellation Ursa Minor, the Little Bear.

URSA MAJOR & THE PLOUGH

The Plough, or Seven Stars, is not actually a constellation but the brightest part of the constellation Ursa Major, the Big Bear. The most important thing about the Plough is that some of its stars make useful signposts to other parts of the sky.

BOOTES

The three left-hand stars of the Plough can be used to trace a gentle curve downward to the bright orange star Arcturus in the constellation Bootes, the Herdsman.

CASSIOPEIA

CEPHEUS

DRACO

Polaris

URSA MINOR

Dubhe

Mizar

Merak

BOOTES

URSA MAJOR

Arcturus

LEO

LEO

Directly underneath the Plough is the constellation Leo, the Lion. It is one of the few constellations that bears even the slightest resemblance to its name. Its bright star, Regulus, is the dot in an inverted question mark of stars known as the Sickle.

Regulus

EXPLORING SPACE WITH TELESCOPES

England was a maritime nation, and sailors used stars for navigation. So in 1675 King Charles II founded the Royal Observatory at Greenwich. Astronomers were asked to try and find a good way of figuring out the longitude of a location.

Galileo Galilei was the first person to look at the night sky with a telescope, and in doing so, he revolutionized the study of the heavens. Telescopes quickly disproved the old idea of crystal spheres around Earth and revealed an entire universe that waited to be explored. Galileo himself made some important discoveries, including four moons orbiting Jupiter, Saturn's rings, craters on the Moon, individual stars in the Milky Way, and sunspots, from which he figured out that the Sun itself rotated. Refracting telescopes, like Galileo's, and the new reflecting telescopes showed much more detail than naked-eye observation. Bigger telescopes with better lenses enabled astronomers to make more and more discoveries.

HERSCHEL'S 40-FT. TELESCOPE

On March 13, 1781, Sir William Herschel (1738–1822) discovered the planet Uranus, using a 7-ft. (2-m) homemade reflecting telescope. The biggest telescope he built was this 40-ft. (12-m) reflector, but it was awkward to use. The mirror had been made with extra copper and tarnished easily.

GALILEO'S TELESCOPES

Galileo's most powerful telescope could enlarge an image up to 30 times. This is around the same magnification as a pair of modern binoculars. These telescopes are refracting telescopes, which means that they have lenses at each end of a tube, giving the best magnification.

GALILEO'S BELIEFS

Galileo Galilei (1564–1642) was an Italian mathematician, physicist, and astronomer who came into conflict with the Roman Catholic Church because he supported Copernicus' heliocentric theory. He was forbidden to teach the new ideas, and then, when it became clear that he had not changed his mind, he was tried by the Inquisition. Threatened with torture, he publicly recanted, though privately he still believed Copernicus.

NEWTON'S TELESCOPE

Sir Isaac Newton (1642–1727) was an English physicist and mathematician known for figuring out the law of gravity. He also designed an easy-to-use reflecting telescope in 1668. A reflecting telescope uses a shaped mirror to reflect and magnify images.

SPACE
-A TIMELINE-

~1543~
Copernicus publishes De revolutionibus. He states that Earth circles the Sun

~1575–1580~
Istanbul Observatory built

~1610~
Galileo looks at the sky through a telescope

~1668~
Isaac Newton builds his reflecting telescope

~1675~
Greenwich Observatory founded

~1781~
William Herschel discovers the planet Uranus

~1845~
Lord Rosse, using the "Leviathan of Parsonstown" telescope, finds that nebulae have a spiral shape

~1846~
J.G. Galle in Berlin finds the planet Neptune, as predicted by John Couch Adams in England and Urbain Le Verrier in France

SPIRALING NEBULAE

To study nebulae, William Parsons, the Earl of Rosse, built a gigantic reflecting telescope in the grounds of his castle in Parsonstown, Ireland. In 1845, Rosse discovered that some of the nebulae were a spiral shape. His drawing of the nebula M51 was very accurate when it was later compared with photographs.

Rosse's drawing of the nebula M51

Photograph of the nebula M51

SISTERLY LOVE

In 1772, Herschel brought his sister Caroline from Hanover to England to help him. When she was not acting as her brother's secretary and assistant, Caroline watched the sky with her own telescope, looking for comets. By 1797, she had found eight.

Tricks & Techniques

In 1609, the Italian astronomer Galileo revolutionized astronomy when he used a home-made telescope to view the heavens. Today, astronomers can launch probes into the depths of the solar system to send back new information, while space telescopes feed back huge amounts of data on the stars and galaxies. Although there are many kinds of telescope, they are all built to do two things—to collect as much light as possible and to provide the most detailed images. Both of these properties depend on the size of the collecting lens or mirror.

SPACE PROBES

Unfortunately it will not be possible for humans to visit many parts of the solar system because of the extreme dangers involved. However, it has been possible for astronomers to send robotic probes to planets in the solar system and beyond. These probes relay images to Earth via radio signals from TV cameras, while other onboard instruments take a range of measurements.

RADIO TELESCOPES

Radio telescopes were first used in the 1940s to detect radio signals from space. Many objects in the universe, from stars to galaxies, emit radio waves. Because radio waves are longer than light waves, radio telescopes need to be bigger than ordinary telescopes to capture the same amount of detail. Radio waves can penetrate through dust clouds that block visible light, and have been used to map the Milky Way.

visible light

radio waves → infra-red

microwaves

ultra violet

X-ray

gamma rays

wavelength increases

SCIENCE EXPLAINED:
THE ELECTROMAGNETIC SPECTRUM

Light is a form of radiation that is transported in waves. Each of the colors of the rainbow has its own wavelength. The entire range of wavelengths is called the electromagnetic spectrum. Unfortunately, the protective atmosphere of Earth cuts out many of the wavelengths, but from space, the entire spectrum is visible. By studying what kind of radiation is emitted from objects such as stars, astronomers can learn about an object's density, temperature, chemical composition, and how it moves.

HUBBLE SPACE TELESCOPE

Space telescopes have revolutionized astronomy. The protective atmosphere of Earth is a menace to astronomers, because it causes the image we see through a telescope to quiver and ripple like the surface of a pond. It is this that makes the stars twinkle. In space, however, there is no atmosphere. Launched in 1990, the Hubble Space Telescope orbits about 370 mi (600km) above the Earth, sending back startlingly clear images to astronomers.

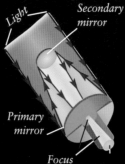

REFLECTING TELESCOPES

Today, most telescopes built for research use mirrors to collect the light. Mirrors have several advantages over lenses. Whereas lenses create false colors, absorb light, and can sag under their own weight, mirrors do not have such handicaps.

Light

Secondary mirror

Primary mirror

Focus

1. Light falls through the top of the open-frame tube, and heads towards the primary mirror.

2. The light is reflected up the tube to the smaller, secondary mirror.

3. The light is reflected back down the tube, through a hole in the primary, to the focus (located beneath the primary).

REFRACTING TELESCOPES

Refracting telescopes consist of two lenses—one at the front (the objective lens) and one at the back (the eyepiece, that magnifies the focused image). Today, these are less popular with professional astronomers than reflecting telescopes. Binoculars, which are popular with amateur astronomers, are twin refracting telescopes arranged side by side.

Objective lens

Focus

Eyepiece

1. The objective lens catches the light and brings it to a focus.

2. The eyepiece magnifies the focused image.

CABBAGE PATCH ROCKETS

The American Robert Goddard (1882–1945) made practical experiments with rockets and different fuels. On March 16, 1926, he launched the first rocket to use a liquid propellant—from his aunt Effie's cabbage patch!

FROM FICTION TO FACT

Early rocket pioneers were inspired by two adventure stories by the Frenchman Jules Verne. In *De la Terre à la Lune* (1865) and *Autour de la Lune* (1870), he describes the adventures of his three-man crew, launched into space by cannon. Now that men have been to the Moon, amazing similarities between the real moonshots and Verne's stories can be seen. For example, his launch took place in Florida, near Cape Kennedy. This is near the equator, where the speed of Earth's rotation is at its greatest and helps a rocket escape Earth's gravity more easily. Verne's cannon was called the *Columbiad*. The command module of *Apollo 11* was named *Columbia*. Verne even described a test flight using animals in a scaled-down model.

LAUNCH VEHICLES

Ariane is the rocket used as a launch vehicle by the European Space Agency, ESA. Many satellites, as well as the Giotto probe, have been launched by *Ariane*. When a rocket is fired, the burning propellants make hot gases that expand and escape from the base of the rocket. This force, called thrust, lifts the rocket off the ground.

OVERCOMING GRAVITY

Konstantin Tsiolkovsky (1857–1935) studied math, physics, and astronomy. Inspired by Jules Verne's space stories, Tsiolkovsky thought about how to overcome gravity and realized that rockets were the key to space flight. He figured out the basic theory of rocket propulsion, including using liquid propellants and the amount of fuel a rocket would need in order to go into orbit.

WERNHER VON BRAUN

Wernher von Braun (1912–1977) was born in Germany. He helped produce the V2 rocket, which was used as a weapon against Great Britain during World War II. Later, von Braun went to America, where he helped on the space program, including designing the *Saturn V* rocket.

ROCKETS

Exploring space from Earth is strictly limited. We could explore more if we got off Earth. There have been many writers who have imagined that it was possible to do this, but only in the last half of the 1900s has any object been sent into space from Earth. To escape the gravitational pull of Earth, a vehicle has to travel at 25,000 mph (40,200km/h), or 7 mi. (11km) per second. The only engine that can produce this type of energy is a rocket. Rockets were invented by the Chinese around 1150. Their rockets burned gunpowder and were used as weapons. Around 1500, the Chinese scientist Wan Hu tried to fly, using 47 rockets tied to his sedan chair. The rockets exploded, and Wan Hu was never seen again. It was only in 1903 that the Russian mathematician Konstantin Tsiolkovsky suggested using rockets to reach space.

MOON ROCKET

Saturn V, the rocket used to launch the manned *Apollo* spacecraft to the Moon, was the biggest rocket ever built. *Saturn V* was a three-stage rocket. The first stage was powerful enough to lift the rocket from the launchpad. When the fuel was used up, the first stage separated and fell back to Earth. The second stage then fired, and the lighter rocket traveled higher and faster. The third stage lifted the spacecraft into its flightpath.

JAPANESE HOPES

The Japanese NASDA (National Space Development Agency) has space centers in Kagoshima and Tanegashima. Between 1994 and 1999, NASDA launched the H-II rocket, with five successes, to investigate the Sun, the Moon, and Mars.

SPUTNIK & OTHER SATELLITES

On October 4, 1957, the world was thrilled and excited to hear a beeping sound from space. The Soviet Union had launched Sputnik (meaning "traveler"), the first-ever artificial satellite in space. In January 1958, America launched its first satellite, Explorer 1. This was the start of the Space Age. Since then, thousands of satellites have been launched for collecting scientific information, communication, navigation, spying, and weather forecasting, as well as astronomy. Some types of radiation, such as X-rays, infrared, and ultraviolet, cannot penetrate the atmosphere and cannot be studied from Earth. Astronomical satellites above Earth's atmosphere can work without interference.

POLLUTION CHECKS

The American space agency NASA (the National Aeronautics and Space Administration) planned a "Mission to Planet Earth" program of satellites. Responding to concerns about pollution, the first satellite in the series was the Upper Atmosphere Research Satellite, launched in 1991. It checks changes in the ozone layer.

SPUTNIK

Sputnik 1 was a steel sphere weighing 184 lbs. (84kg), with a diameter of 23 in. (58cm). Sputnik orbited Earth once every 96 minutes, 17 seconds, traveling at heights varying from 142 mi. (228km) to 589 mi. (947km). It sent out radio signals for 21 days.

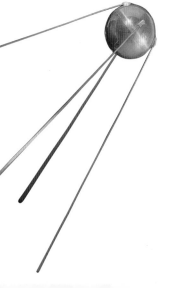

SMALL BUT POWERFUL

Explorer 1, America's first satellite, orbited Earth for 12 years, collecting information on temperatures, meteorites, and cosmic rays. It discovered the Van Allen radiation belt, 600 mi. (1,000km) above Earth. Over a period of 30 years, 55 Explorer scientific satellites were launched.

TELSTAR

The first communications satellite was Telstar 1. Built in America by the Bell Telephone Company, it was launched in 1962. It used microwave radiation and solar power to relay telephone and radio signals. It also had a TV channel, which was used to make the first live broadcast from the U.S.A. to Europe.

SPACE
-A TIMELINE-

~1865, 1870~

Jules Verne publishes his two inspirational novels De la Terre à la Lune (From the Earth to the Moon) *and* Autour de la Lune (Round the Moon)

~1903~

Konstantin Tsiolkovsy publishes his theory of rocket propulsion in The Exploration of Cosmic Space by Means of Reaction Devices

~1919~

Robert Goddard publishes the results of his rocket experiments, including his belief that a rocket could reach the Moon, in A Method of Reaching Extreme Altitudes

SPACE RACERS!

Verney and Gordy, two rhesus monkeys, took part in research on blood flow in space. They were launched along with rats, newts, insects, and plants in a joint Soviet–American biospace mission. They returned to Earth successfully one week later.

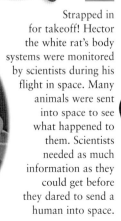

RATS

Strapped in for takeoff! Hector the white rat's body systems were monitored by scientists during his flight in space. Many animals were sent into space to see what happened to them. Scientists needed as much information as they could get before they dared to send a human into space.

LOST IN SPACE

Sputnik 2 carried a dog named Laika into space. Tests showed that she had not been affected by the launch or by being weightless. However, it was not possible to bring the satellite back, and Laika died in space.

MISSION BADGE

The first men on the Moon wore this badge, designed by Michael Collins. It shows an American bald eagle landing on the Moon with an olive branch in its talons. The sunshine on Earth in the background is coming from the wrong direction—it should light the top, not the side.

FLYING THE FLAG

While Michael Collins flew the Command Module in orbit around the Moon, Edwin "Buzz" Aldrin *(left and above)* and Neil Armstrong landed on the surface, in the Sea of Tranquility, on July 20, 1969. The American flag is wired to hold it out as though the wind is blowing it.

EVERLASTING

There is no wind on the Moon, so Neil Armstrong's footprint—the first on the Moon—will last forever.

FAR SIDE OF THE MOON

Until this picture was taken by *Luna 3*, humans had never seen the far side of the Moon. As it orbits Earth, the Moon rotates, keeping the same side facing us.

MOONSHOTS

The Moon is our closest neighbor in space, orbiting the planet at a distance of around 221,456 mi. (384,403km). Only 12 men have ever walked on it. For mankind's first journey into space, the Moon was the obvious place to aim for. Soviet *Luna* probes were the first to reach the Moon. *Luna 2* crash-landed on the Moon, and *Luna 3* took the first-ever photograph of the far side of the Moon. In May 1961, American Alan Shepard went into space for 15 minutes. In a speech to congress, President John F. Kennedy challenged the nation to put a man on the Moon before the end of the decade. America succeeded and made six Moon landings.

THE RACE TO SPACE

The goal of putting a man on the Moon was a huge challenge for American scientists. Enthusiasm for the project was enormous, and the desire to beat the Soviet Union was very strong. As a result, America put men on the Moon in less than ten years. *Apollo 11*, carrying the first astronauts to land on the Moon, was launched on July 16, 1969.

LUNOKHOD

Lunokhod was a roving vehicle sent to the Moon in the unmanned Soviet probe *Luna 17*, launched in 1970. It was driven by remote control from Earth. Television cameras on the front allowed scientists to explore the Moon.

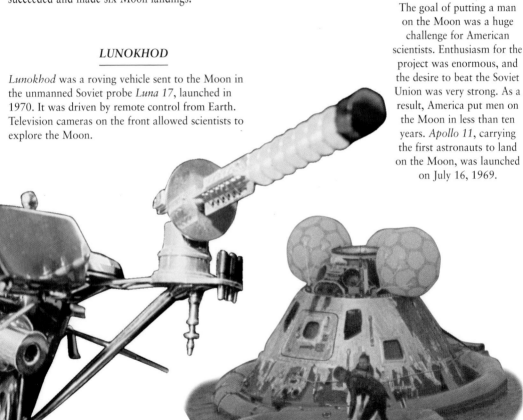

RETURN TO EARTH

Bringing astronauts back to Earth is just as complicated and dangerous as sending them off. The *Apollo* Command Modules landed in the Pacific Ocean. A flotation collar stopped them from sinking. Divers from waiting navy ships rushed to the modules to help the astronauts out.

ASTRONAUTS

To fly a vehicle into space requires a highly trained group of men and women. Astronauts must be fit enough to cope with the physical demands of weightlessness, and they also have to be able to understand the technical complexities of the spacecraft and its instruments. The first astronauts also had to be small enough to fit into little spacecraft. To date, only around 480 astronauts have traveled into space, but only 26 have ventured farther than a low Earth orbit.

FIRST FOR WOMEN

Valentina Tereshkova (b.1937) was the first woman in space. She orbited Earth 45 times in *Vostok* 6, which was launched on June 16, 1963, and Tereshkova returned to Earth by parachute on June 19. Before she volunteered for space training, Tereshkova was a textile worker who enjoyed parachute jumping as a hobby.

JOHN GLENN

John Glenn (b.1921), seen here undergoing respiratory testing as part of his training, was the first American to orbit Earth on February 20, 1962. He landed in the Atlantic Ocean after a frightening re-entry in which burning pieces of the capsule flew past his window.

FOOD FOR THOUGHT

Astronauts in space need to eat! Food is packed in individual portions, and on the *Apollo* missions, it was freeze-dried, like this pack of beef and vegetables. Hot or cold water was added, and the astronauts then had to suck it out of the packet. Today, the shuttle has an oven. Drinks are drunk through special mouthpieces to stop drops from escaping and floating around the spacecraft.

FIRST IN SPACE

Yuri Gagarin (1934–1968), the first man in space, was a pilot in the Soviet Union's Air Force who had volunteered for space training. Gagarin orbited Earth once on April 12, 1961, in a *Vostock* spacecraft. He returned to Earth by ejecting from the spacecraft and using a parachute to fall the last 2.5 mi. (4km) to land. Until this flight, no one knew whether humans would be able to adapt to conditions in space. Overnight, Gagarin became world famous. He was training for a flight in the new *Soyuz* spacecraft when his MiG-15 aircraft crashed, killing him.

WORKING IN SPACE

To go outside a spacecraft in space, an astronaut must wear a protective suit. In the 1980s, astronauts used a Manned Maneuvering Unit (MMU), which was a jet-propelled backpack (*left*). It allowed astronauts to move around in space and return to their spacecraft. Since then, the Simplified Aid for EVA Rescue has been used, allowing for greater mobility. Astronauts on board the International Space Station (ISS) all use these suits.

SPACE
-A TIMELINE-

~1925~
Edwin Hubble proves that the Andromeda Nebula is not part of the Milky Way, but a separate galaxy

~1930~
Clyde Tombaugh in the U.S.A. finds the planet Pluto, now considered a dwarf planet

~1932~
Karl Jansky discovers radio signals coming from space

~1949~
Radio signals discovered to come from stars and other heavenly bodies

~1957~
Sputnik 1, the first satellite, launched by the Soviet Union

~1958~
Explorer 1, the U.S.A.'s first satellite, is launched

~1961~
April 12: Yuri Gagarin, of the Soviet Union, is the first man in space

THE MERCURY SEVEN

Seven American pilots were chosen for training as the first astronauts. They were (*back row from left*) Alan Shepard, Virgil "Gus" Grissom, Gordon Cooper, (*front row from left*) Walter Schira, Donald "Deke" Slayton, John Glenn and Scott Carpenter. Americans were shocked when the Soviet Union got a man into space first. Plans to send an American into space were quickly brought forward.
Alan Shepard, in a *Mercury* space capsule, landed in the Atlantic Ocean after a flight of 15 minutes on May 5, 1961.

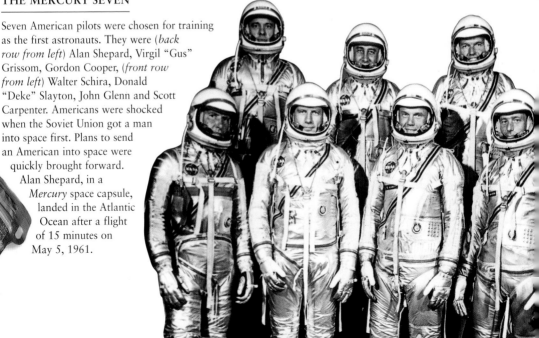

Journeys Toward the Sun

Humans have only managed to travel a very short distance in space. In order to find out more about the solar system and the bodies in it, space probes are used. A probe is a robot explorer equipped with instruments for measuring, studying, recording, experimenting, and photographing. A space probe may take years to reach its destination, and many have not succeeded in their task because of mechanical failure. Those that do succeed can travel past heavenly bodies on their way, taking pictures and collecting information that they transmit back to Earth. The first space probes were sent to the Moon and to Venus, the closest planet to Earth. From 1960 onward, the Soviet Union sent a series of 18 *Venera* probes to Venus. Huge atmospheric pressure and intense heat destroyed many of the probes, although some of them survived long enough to send back useful information. The American probe *Mariner 2* reached Venus in 1962. Between them, the probes collected enormous amounts of information.

CLOUDS ON VENUS

Photographs from space, like this one taken by *Mariner 10*, show the thick cloudy atmosphere that covers Venus. Although the planet rotates slowly, with a retrograde orbit (it moves in the opposite direction to other planets), the clouds move quickly. They only take four days to circle the planet. They are very dense and are made up of drops of sulfuric acid and gases such as carbon dioxide.

GIOTTO

Giotto was launched by ESA in 1985, using their *Ariane* rocket. It encountered Halley's Comet in 1986. It came within 376 mi. (605km) of the core of the comet, showing it to be peanut-shaped, dark, and cratered. As well as *Giotto*, the Soviet Union and Japan sent probes to rendezvous with Halley's Comet.

MISSION CONTROL

Every probe is monitored at all times from the ground. Many people work at Mission Control, sending instructions to a spacecraft and working on the information that it sends back. Mission Control is an essential part of any operation that takes place in space.

SUN SPOTTING

Without our star, the Sun, there would be no life on Earth. From the earliest times, people have been interested in the Sun and how it works. *Ulysses* was built by ESA and launched from the shuttle *Discovery* in October 1990. It was designed to orbit the Sun over the Sun's poles. It examined the solar wind and the particles that make it up.

MAGELLAN PROBE

In 1989, NASA sent the *Magellan* probe to Venus. Using radar, it has been able to map most of the surface of the planet. The information that it collected has allowed scientists to make a 3-D computer model of the surface. They have discovered that Venus is covered in volcanoes.

MERCURY

Mariner 10 made three flybys of Mercury, the planet closest to the Sun. It is the only space probe to have visited Mercury. Launched in 1973, *Mariner* was protected from the fierce heat of the Sun by a shade and thermal wrappings. *Mariner* sent back 8,000 photographs that showed Mercury's surface was covered with craters, like the Moon. *Mariner 10* also discovered that temperatures on Mercury range from 800°F (420°C) to –300°F (–180°C) and that it has a very thin atmosphere.

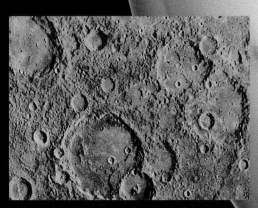

Journeys Away from the Sun

Most of the planets in the solar system are farther away from the Sun than Earth is. The planets Mars, Jupiter, and Saturn have been known to astronomers since ancient times. Uranus was only discovered in 1781, and Neptune was found in 1846. The farthest reaches of the solar system are still largely unexplored. Only in 1989 did *Voyager 2* reach and observe the planet Neptune, passing 3,000 mi. (4,950km) above its north pole. Mars is the second-closest planet to Earth and many Soviet, American, and Japanese probes have been launched to explore it. The *Pioneer* and *Voyager* probes have, between them, visited Jupiter, Saturn, Uranus, and Neptune.

LOOKING AT MARS

Mariner 9 was launched in 1971 and orbited Mars. It was the first probe to orbit a planet. It took 6,876 photos of the surface. These showed volcanoes, including Olympus Mons, the biggest volcano in the solar system. Mariner found channels such as dried-up riverbeds, but it found no sign of vegetation. The probe also took photographs of Mars's two moons, Phobos and Deimos.

NEXT STOP, SATURN

The *Cassini-Huygens* probe to Saturn was launched by NASA in 1997. It arrived in 2004, and looks set to remain until 2017, passing all the larger moons in a series of 63 orbits. On board *Cassini* is the ESA probe *Huygens*, which was launched into the atmosphere of the moon Titan in 2005. In its 90 minutes on Titan, *Huygens* sent back photographs and data.

RINGS AND MOONS

Saturn has been visited by several probes, *Pioneer 11*, *Voyagers 1* and *2*, and *Cassini-Huygens*. They found that its rings were made up of millions of tiny chunks of ice, rock, and dust. There are hundreds of narrow rings 0.6 mi. (1km) thick. Some are circular, some are oval, and at least one is crooked. Saturn has at least 62 moons! The planet itself has a strong magnetic field and a very low density.

DISCOVERING NEPTIUNE

Voyager 2 was able to visit four planets due to a rare alignment of planets. They were so positioned that on its journey from Earth, *Voyager 2* could use the gravity of each planet to push it farther into space. Launched in 1977, the probe took 12 years to reach Neptune, where it discovered a huge storm called the Great Dark Spot. It also discovered six moons and four very faint rings.

MARS PATHFINDER, OR CARL SAGAN MEMORIAL STATION

The *Mars Pathfinder* probe sent a craft to the surface of Mars in 1997. The lander released the robot microrover, *Sojourner*. There, it analyzed a rock nicknamed Yogi. Originally intended to explore Mars for 30 days, *Pathfinder* kept going three times longer. NASA finally lost touch with it in March 1998.

BY JUPITER!

Pioneer 10 was launched in March 1972 and encountered Jupiter in December 1973. It was the first probe to travel beyond Mars, and the first to navigate the asteroid belt. *Pioneer 10* took the first close-up pictures of Jupiter. It could not find any solid surface on the planet and also discovered that Jupiter has a magnetic field 2,000 times stronger than Earth's.

SPACE
-A TIMELINE-

~1961~
May 5: Alan Shepard is the first American in space

May 25: President Kennedy challenges the U.S.A. to put a man on the Moon within ten years

~1962~
Telstar, the world's first commercial satellite, is launched

~1963~
Arecibo radio telescope is built

~1969~
July 16: Apollo 11 is launched on its journey to the Moon

July 20: Neil Armstrong is the first man on the Moon

~1975~
Very Large Array first used

~1977~
Voyagers 1 and 2 launched

~1980~
Voyager 1 encounters Saturn, then leaves the solar system

~1981~
First space shuttle flight (shuttle Columbia)

~1986~
Giotto encounters Halley's Comet

Challenger disaster: space shuttle blows up 73 seconds after launch

First part of space station Mir placed in orbit

MISSION BADGE

Every shuttle flight has a mission badge. This badge, showing the mission number and names of the crew; was worn for the last American linkup with the Russian space station Mir, in June 1998. The mission included the delivery of supplies to the space station and the bringing home of the American astronaut Andrew Thomas.

LIFTOFF!

The shuttle is launched like a rocket. It is attached to an external fuel tank and two rocket boosters. Two minutes after launch, when the shuttle is 28 mi. (45km) above Earth, the boosters fall away. They land by parachute in the sea and are collected to use again. Eight minutes after launch, the fuel in the external tank is used up. It falls away but is not recovered.

PIGGYBACK SHUTTLE

NASA uses a specially adapted Boeing 747 jumbo jet to move shuttles around the United States. The shuttle rides piggyback on the 747 because it has not been designed to take off in level flight like an airplane.

ICE

The shuttle *Challenger* exploded 73 seconds after its launch on January 28, 1986, killing all seven crew members. It was the worst accident ever to happen in space. Ice on the launchpad had damaged one of the shuttle's solid rocket boosters, and hot gas burned into the fuel tank. The liquid gas that poured out ignited at once, causing a gigantic explosion.

THE SPACE SHUTTLE

Sending probes and satellites into space using rockets is extremely expensive. To reduce the cost, NASA esigned a reusable spacecraft—the shuttle. It is expected that the space shuttle program will be retired in 2011. The shuttle is used to launch, retrieve, and repair satellites. It is also used as a laboratory during the 14 days that it can stay in orbit. Each shuttle mission has a commander, a pilot, and a number of other specialists, some of whom perform spacewalks, and undertake scientific experiments on board.

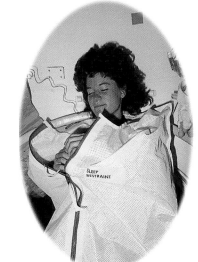

IN CONTROL

All the controls for the space shuttle are located in the cockpit. There are controls for flying the shuttle, controls for all the systems in the shuttle such as air and power, and controls for external operations, and the cargo in the payload bay. The commander sits in the left-hand seat in the cockpit looking forward, and the pilot sits in the right-hand seat.

SWEET DREAMS

In space there is no down or up, so astronauts can sleep anywhere. Sally Ride, the first female American astronaut, is seen (*above*) in a sleeping bag that is attached to the sides of the craft. This prevents her from floating around. She knows she will wake up in the same place!

SMOOTH LANDINGS

When it is ready to return to Earth after a mission, the shuttle uses its engines to brake. As it slows, it falls toward Earth. As it falls through the atmosphere, the shuttle heats up and the air around it glows. The hot air stops the radios working from for around ten minutes. The crew is protected from the heat by the shuttle's coat of ceramic tiles. Closer to the ground, the shuttle uses wing and tail flaps and a parachute to slow it down further. Then it lands like a glider.

TELESCOPES TODAY

A great deal of astronomical exploration and fact-finding is still done with Earth-based telescopes. Satellites have provided a wealth of information, but most of them are looking at one object, such as the Sun, or are only working in a particular area of radiation, such as X-rays. Astronomers today use optical telescopes housed in observatories built in high, dry places where there is a clear atmosphere and no light pollution. Most optical telescopes are big reflectors, attached to cameras and controlled by computers. Radio waves coming from bodies in space were first noticed in 1932, but radio telescopes were not developed until after World War II. Radio telescopes listen rather than look. They collect weaker signals than optical telescopes, so they can explore much farther out in space. Radio telescopes have found radio sources such as pulsars and quasars in the heavens and detected objects 13,000, 000,000 light-years away from Earth.

COMPUTERIZED ASTRONOMERS

Professional astronomers rarely look through telescopes! Most of their work is done on computers. This astronomer works on images received by signals from a radio telescope. The observatory, at Plateau de Bure in France, has five dishes and explores pulsars—stars that are the source of very regular radio signals— in distant galaxies.

BIG BANG

Satellite telescopes have opened up a huge new range of space for astronomers to explore. One question that they are eager to answer is how the universe began. The Big Bang theory proposes that it started with a gigantic explosion around 15,000,000,000 years ago. COBE, the Cosmic Background Explorer, was launched in 1989 to study the microwave radiation that can be found very faintly everywhere in the universe. COBE discovered that it rippled, as it would do if it were the remains of the Big Bang.

THE VERY LARGE ARRAY

A radio telescope has an antenna in a dish. Radio waves from space, sent from a natural body like a star or from a human-made spacecraft, are bounced off the dish, collected by the antenna, and converted into electronic signals that can be "read" by a computer. Several radio telescopes can be used together like one large one. This allows astronomers to collect signals from far away in space and to get more detailed images than they can get from optical telescopes. The Very Large Array, in New Mexico, has 27 movable dishes, each one with a diameter of 82 ft. (25m).

MAUNA KEA

Many countries, including the U.S.A., the U.K., Canada, and France, have optical telescopes at observatories on the Mauna Kea volcano in Hawaii. At a height of 14,000 ft. (4,270km), they are above one third of Earth's atmosphere. As well as giving clearer pictures, the observatories stay cool. It is important that the instruments are not affected by temperature changes, as this distorts the image.

SOHO

SOHO—the Solar Heliospheric Observatory—is a satellite launched by ESA that orbits the Sun. It has 12 instruments that study the solar atmosphere and how the Sun is made up. An ultraviolet camera photographs the Sun at four different temperatures each day. SOHO's photographs have recorded activity such as massive explosions and a sunquake with seismic waves 2 mi. (3km) high traveling at 250,000 mph (400,000km/h).

284 angstroms

195 angstroms

171 angstroms

304 angstroms

AMATEUR ASTRONOMY

Many amateur astronomers enjoy watching the heavens and heavenly bodies as a hobby. Some collect information that is useful to professional astronomers. Many comets have been found and have had their orbits constantly monitored by amateur astronomers.

SPACE
-A TIMELINE-

~1989~

Voyager 2 *encounters* Neptune, *then leaves the solar system*

~1990~

Hubble Space Telescope launched

~1993~

Hubble Space Telescope repaired on space shuttle

~1995~

Galileo *probe visits Jupiter*

~1997~

Mars Pathfinder *sends a lander, including robot microrover* Sojourner, *to the surface of Mars*

Cassini/Huygens *probe launched.* Cassini *due to encounter Saturn in 2004,* Huygens *due to descend into Titan's atmosphere in 2005*

~1998~

Russians announce that space station Mir will be decommissioned in 2001.

THE HUBBLE SPACE TELESCOPE

The Hubble Space Telescope is a satellite built by NASA and ESA and launched in 1990. It is a reflecting telescope and also works in ultraviolet. The satellite receives power from two solar panels. The volume of space Hubble can cover is 350 times bigger than can be seen from Earth. It is designed to look a long way beyond the solar system and to collect information about how stars and galaxies evolve. The Hubble Space Telescope was designed to be repaired as necessary by shuttle astronauts. So far, five repair missions have taken place, It is still going strong and expected to continue until 2014.

HUBBLE TELESCOPE

When the Hubble Space Telescope was launched, scientists were horrified to discover that the images it sent back to Earth were blurred. They discovered that its 96-in. (2.4-m) main mirror had been ground to the wrong shape. Although it was less than a hair's width wrong, it was enough to cause NASA great embarrassment. However, this was fixed in 1993.

EDWIN HUBBLE

Edwin Hubble (1889–1953), after whom the Hubble Space Telescope was named, was an American astronomer who was interested in nebulae and galaxies. He proved that our galaxy, the Milky Way, was not the only galaxy.

HUBBLE OPTICS

Satellites are built in sterile, temperature-controlled atmospheres, as dust or temperature changes could ruin the working of delicate instruments. Grinding mirrors and making lenses for telescopes requires great accuracy. The making of the optical parts of the Hubble Space Telescope was carried out with extreme care.

TO THE RESCUE

The space shuttle *Endeavour* was launched in 1993 on a mission to repair the telescope. Two astronauts caught the telescope and hauled it into the shuttle's payload bay, using the robot Remote Manipulator Arm. The solar panels were replaced. The Wide Field Planetary Camera was replaced, and the faulty lens was corrected. Other instruments were checked or updated. The repairs took 35 hours of spacewalks and were completely successful.

BEFORE AND AFTER

These two pictures show how much improvement there was to photographs after the Hubble Space Telescope was repaired. On the left is a photograph of the M100 galaxy taken with the faulty lens. On the right is the same galaxy taken with the repaired lens. Astronomers can now see star clusters and individual stars. M100 is tens of millions of light-years away and is found in the constellation Virgo.

MIR

Space station Mir is built of several sections, or modules. Each has a different purpose. The core module contains the main living cabin while other modules contain laboratories and docking ports. Solar panels stick out in all directions. Space shuttle *Atlantis* uses a special docking adapter to connect to the space station.

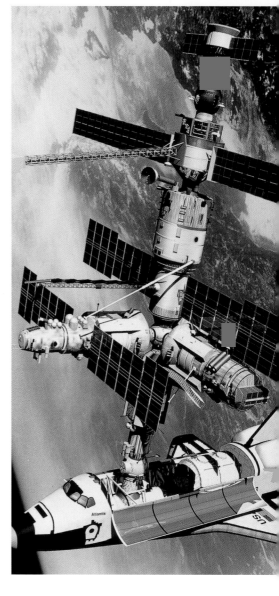

IN A SPIN

An American schoolchild suggested an experiment to see if spiders could spin webs in space. Spiders Anita and Arabella flew on Skylab. Being in free fall confused Arabella, and she could not spin a web correctly for the first two days. Anita was not allowed to spin for several days. She could make good webs at once when she was allowed to start.

RENDEZVOUS

The year 1995 saw the start of a two-year program in which America and Russia worked together in space. Russian cosmonauts flew in the shuttle *Atlantis*, and American astronauts worked on space station Mir. At their first meeting, the two crews posed in the spacelab module in *Atlantis*' payload bay for this group photograph. Mir commander Vladimir Dezhurov is on the left, behind the man with crossed arms. *Atlantis* commander Robert "Hoot" Gibson is upside down, top right—around the position of one o'clock.

SPACE STATIONS

A space station is an enormous satellite. It is so big that astronauts can live and work in it for much longer than they could on a spacecraft. There have been several Soviet space stations: nine named Salyut and the current Russian one, which is named Mir. America has had one space station, Skylab, and ESA built one named Spacelab, which is used in the space shuttle's payload bay. On a space station, longer and more complicated experiments can be carried out than on other craft. This is very important for future space exploration. Valuable information has been gathered on how humans cope with long spells of weightlessness. Astronauts from many countries have also worked on such things as making drugs in very pure forms to help sick people on Earth.

DOOR TO DOOR DELIVERY

Astronauts look out of the windows as *Atlantis* arrives at Mir to deliver supplies. This mission included the delivery of a docking module. Docking the space shuttle with space station Mir took careful maneuvering, as Mir orbits Earth at a speed of 17,000 mph (27,000km/h).

WEIGHTLESSNESS

Being in free fall, or weightless, in space looks fun, as Skylab astronauts Edward Gibson (*floating*) and Gerald Carr demonstrate. But weightlessness produces medical problems. Astronauts who live on space stations have to exercise for up to three hours every day to try and keep fit. They also take extra vitamins and calcium. Soviet cosmonauts have worked on *Mir* for more than one year, but no one yet knows what would happen to someone traveling in space for a very long time.

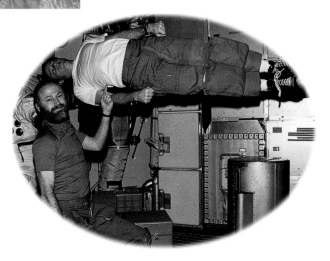

KEEPING CLEAN

Astronauts on board Skylab used a shower that pulled up and sealed around the astronaut's body. Water was air-blasted through a handheld shower head and then vacuumed off—similar to drying yourself with a vacuum! The shower leaked, so now on the shuttle astronauts have sponge baths, using a wash basin.

DEADLY HOLES

Sometimes a supernova explosion leaves behind a remnant that is too massive even for a neutron star. When this happens, the star disappears altogether and becomes a black hole. The nucleus gets crushed into such a tiny volume that the extreme gravitational pull of the core closes up the space around it, preventing even light from escaping. Black holes cannot be seen, but their presence can be detected because they swallow surrounding matter. The matter spirals into the black hole and forms a disc that gets so hot that it emits X-rays. These can be detected by space probes. As you approach a black hole you start to feel its gravitational pull get stronger. The closer you get, the more speed you will need to escape its tight clutches. If you were foolhardy enough to enter the barrier of blackness known as the "event horizon," you would never get out again. If you were really reckless and ventured anywhere near the center, you would be sucked out of existence!

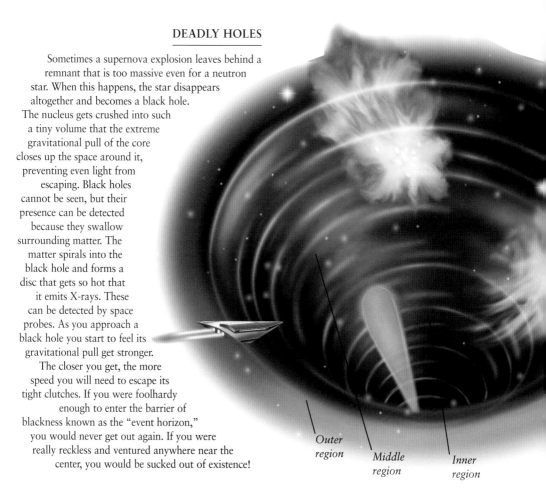

Outer region

Middle region

Inner region

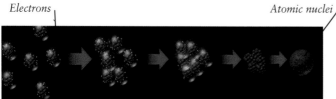

Electrons

Atomic nuclei

NEUTRON STARS

Neutron stars are born when gravity forces a star to collapse to such an extent that its electrons are forced together inside the atomic nuclei (*see above*). The resulting neutron star can be as small as 19 mi. (30km) across. They have intense magnetic fields and spin very quickly, some at more than a hundred times per second. Neutron stars are also intensely magnetic. These two factors cause them to emit their light in the form of two beams on opposite sides of the star (*right*). Neutron stars whose beams we can see are called pulsars.

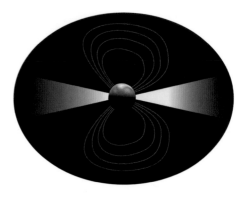

Cosmic Puzzlers

When stars like the Sun die, they end their days as white dwarfs. Stars that start out ten times bigger than the Sun, however, face a very different fate. The remnants left by such explosions are far denser than white dwarfs and can become either small superdense objects called neutron stars or black holes. Black holes suck matter out of the universe, like vast whirlpools. Even stranger are wormholes. They are thought to link parts of the universe by time tunnels that might conceivably make time travel possible.

EXPLOSION

Supergiant stars rush through their fuel supply and die in a cataclysmic explosion that outshines a billion Suns. Two things happen during a supernova explosion. First, the outer shell of gas is blasted away, as shown in this picture of the Crab Nebula (*above*). There is also an inward implosion, which compresses the star's core to even higher densities than those of white dwarfs. At this point the core will become either a neutron star or a black hole.

TIME TO TRAVEL

Many science fiction films explore the possiblity of time travel. In *The Terminator*, a deadly robot is sent back in time by an evil dictatorship to try to kill a woman who will give birth to the leader of a rebel army. Although this is science fantasy, some astronomers believe that time travel might theoretically be possible because of the existence of space phenomena called wormholes. These are supposed to connect distant parts of the universe by a kind of tunnel in space-time. Just like in a black hole, time slows to a standstill, and the known laws of the universe stop working. If a wormhole could be kept open long enough, it might be possible to travel through unharmed.

MAKING CONTACT

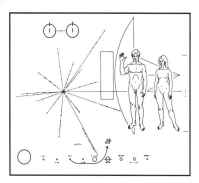

PICTURES INTO SPACE

Two *Pioneer* space probes, numbers *10* and *11*, had an extra mission. After their work exploring the asteroids, Jupiter, and Saturn, they headed for deep space. Each probe has an identical plaque on the outside, engraved with symbols. They show a hydrogen atom, the Sun giving off radio energy, a diagram of the solar system showing which planet *Pioneer* came from, and a male and female figure in front of an outline of *Pioneer* to the same scale.

There are millions of stars in millions of galaxies. Scientists believe there must be many planets orbiting the stars. They hope that life may have evolved on some of them. It is possible that some of that life might be intelligent. Earth has sent messages into space, hoping to make contact. Space is huge, and we have only developed the technology to get in touch in the last 40 years. Attempts have also been made to see if anyone has tried to get in touch with us. Since the early days of radio astronomy, scientists have been interested in finding radio signals that have been sent out deliberately. In 1992, NASA launched a program called SETI (Search for Extra-Terrestrial Intelligence). Nearby stars are being searched and the entire sky scanned for microwaves. Radio telescopes around the world are studying the closest 1,000 stars. So far, no contact has been made in either direction.

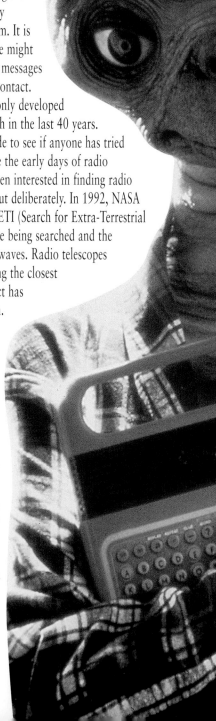

CROP CIRCLES

Have intelligent beings from space ever visited Earth? Some people think that they have. Crop circles, and other geometric shapes, appear from time to time in fields of wheat and other plants. These circles are especially found on the chalk downlands of Salisbury Plain in southern England. There is usually no obvious path connecting them with a human access point. One theory about them is that they are made by beings from space who want to communicate with us. Other theories include local climatic disturbances, herds of madly rotating hedgehogs, and ordinary vandals!

LONG-DISTANCE MESSAGE

The radio telescope in Arecibo is the world's biggest. It is built into a hollow in the hills of Puerto Rico and uses Earth's rotation to sweep the skies. In 1974, astronomers sent a message from Arecibo out into space. The message took three minutes to send, and was directed toward the M13 galaxy in the constellation Hercules. It will take 25,000 years to travel to M13!

CLOSE ENCOUNTERS

The idea that Earth has been visited by beings from space has inspired many movies. Steven Spielberg gave some of the profits he made from the movie *ET* to the SETI Institute for research. It funded META, the Megachannel Extra Terrestrial Assay, which used the 85-ft. (26-m) telescope at Harvard University in Massachusetts for a major search of the northern skies.

GOLD DISKS

The probes *Voyager 1* and *2* explored Jupiter, Saturn, Uranus, and Neptune, and then left the solar system and headed for deep space. Each one carries an identical gold-plated LP record, the "Sounds of Earth." On the record are greetings in 60 languages, animal sounds, natural noises like thunder, the sea and the wind, music, and pictures of life on Earth. There are also instructions on how to play the records.

DESERT PICTURES

In the deserts of southern Peru there are giant images of animals such as a spider, a bird, and a monkey. These Nazca lines are more than 1,000 years old, and some are miles long. They are made by piling up the dark surface stones to show the paler stones beneath. They can only be seen properly from the air but were made long before any known flight.

THE FUTURE

The future for the exploration of space looks very exciting. Many more satellites are planned. The International Space Station (ISS) is almost finished, and it is expected that humans will walk again on the Moon soon. Living on a Moon base would probably happen soon after this. An astronaut on Mars may not be too far away. As the science of space travel develops and becomes ever more sophisticated, who knows what future generations might be able to achieve? Maybe one day we will have the technology to visit all the planets.

TO BOLDLY GO . . .

The imagination of writers and artists has always outrun the abilities of scientists and engineers. Traveling to the stars is a long way away in reality. It is difficult enough to explore the solar system. We have no way of traveling faster than light, which we would have to do in order to reach the stars. But with imaginative creations like *Star Trek*'s Starship Enterprise, we can roam the galaxies.

MOON BASE

In 1998, water ice was discovered at the poles of the Moon. Water on the Moon makes establishing a Moon base a much easier proposition. Ice could be melted into water and used for drinking, washing, and growing plants. It could be turned into oxygen to breathe and hydrogen to use as fuel.

DELTA CLIPPER

One priority for the future is a new space transportation system. The *Delta Clipper* is being tested as one possible successor to the Shuttle. It takes off and lands vertically. Powered by eight rocket engines, it moves from Earth to orbit in only one stage and can carry loads up to 20,000 lbs. (9,070kg) weight. It can be used with or without a crew. Farther into the future, rockets that use nuclear fuel may become possible. They could be used for very long missions.

A SPACE TOILET

"How do you go to the bathroom?" is a question astronauts are often asked. There have been lavatories in space since space station Skylab, which was operational in 1973–1974. The astronaut wears rubber gloves and uses handles and foot rests to hold himself or herself on the seat. Air is used to suck wastes down a funnel into a disposable container. Solid waste is dried and compacted. Wet wipes are used for cleaning both the astronaut and the toilet. This "waste management compartment" was designed by NASA to use on the ISS.

INTERNATIONAL SPACE STATION

In 1998, Russia announced that it was going to decommission the Mir space station, which it did in 2001, after 15 years' service. A new space station is almost finished. It is international, with each of 16 countries in the project building different parts. The International Space Station is finished, but ongoing work and new parts are constantly added. Space shuttles fly engineers, components, and other supplies to the station.

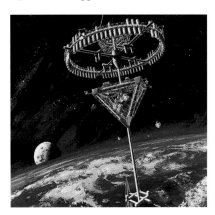

SPACE HOTEL

Spend your vacations in space! The idea of an orbiting hotel has been under investigation by several Japanese companies for many years. The whole complex would be inside, safely sealed away from the freezing vacuum of space.

STATION LIFE

Early space stations look very cluttered, with boxes and equipment everywhere. The new station is designed to have tidy working areas and living quarters. Astronauts each have a cubicle, with storage space, a worktable, computer terminal, and a sleeping bag.

HOW WILL IT ALL END?

What will be the eventual fate of the universe? Everything depends on how dense the universe is. There are three possibilities. If the density is higher than a certain value (the "critical density"), then the universe will eventually stop expanding and collapse in on itself. This is called the Big Crunch Scenario. If the density is less than critical, then the universe will just go on expanding, and the temperature of everything in the universe will plummet. Everything will become freezing cold. This scenario is called the Heat Death Scenario. Finally, if the density is just borderline, the universe will expand less and less but will not collapse. This is called the Flat Universe Scenario. Boomerang *(left)*, a balloon experiment sent high into the atmosphere above the Antarctic, measured the "bumpiness" in the cosmic background. This measurement shows that the universe is actually flat. In other words, neither the Big Crunch nor the Heat Death scenario will happen.

OTHER EVIDENCE

Apart from the expansion of the universe, there are other important pieces of evidence in favour of the Big Bang theory. After any explosion, a fireball expands and cools. In the case of the Big Bang, the original fireball occurred about 15 billion years ago and should by now have a temperature of 270 degrees below zero. The image of the universe taken by the COBE satellite *(right)* confirmed this temperature.

EXPANSION OF THE UNIVERSE

The galaxies all appear to be shooting away from us at very great speeds. This is not because we occupy any special position in the universe—exactly the same thing would be observed from any other galaxy. In fact, it is not the galaxies that are moving, but the space between them that is expanding. Imagine sticking stars on a balloon and then blowing the balloon up. The stars would seem to move apart as the balloon inflates. The expansion of the universe is a process that has been occurring over billions of years.

THE BIG BANG & THE FATE OF THE UNIVERSE

One of the key questions that cosmologists are always trying to solve is how the universe was created. They believe that the universe came into being about 15 billion years ago in a huge explosion named the Big Bang. From being squashed together in a tight ball, matter suddenly expanded outward, eventually creating the stars and planets. Astronomers are also trying to work out how the universe will end, and have come up with a number of different scenarios.

THE BEGINNING OF EVERYTHING

If the universe is expanding, could this mean that the galaxies started out from a dense clump of matter at some time in the past? Imagine filming the explosion of a shell in the air. After the explosion, we see fragments of shell rushing away from one another. If we rewind the film, we will come to the original unexploded shell. Most astronomers now believe that the expansion of the universe started from the explosion of a fireball some 15 billion years ago. This explosion is known as the Big Bang.

CREATING CONDITIONS FOR LIFE

Today, conditions on Earth are perfect for life, allowing a huge diversity of creatures to flourish. However, these conditions have taken billions of years to evolve. Astronomers believe that the universe has gone through several stages since the Big Bang. During the initial fireball the temperature was a staggering 10 billion degrees. After 30,000 years the temperature dropped to 10,000 degrees, still far too hot for life to stand a chance. During this period, called the "radiation era," matter and radiation formed an impenetrable soup. After the radiation era came the "matter era," when matter became separated from the radiation. The universe became transparent and its temperature dropped to the present chilly 270 degrees below zero.

DID YOU KNOW?

Why many amateur astronomers like to watch for comets?
A comet is named for the person who first reports it—this could be you!

Why the first American astronauts had to be less than 5 ft. 11 in. (1.8m) in height?
This was because taller men would not be able to fit into the tiny spacecraft! Astronauts also had to be under 40, physically fit, have a university degree or the equivalent, and be a test pilot with at least 1,500 hours of flying time. The Soviet Union's cosmonauts were even shorter. They had to be under 5 ft. 7 in. (1.7m) tall. They also had to be pilots, fit, and under 30 years of age.

What the word "astronaut" means?
It is Latin for "sailor in the stars."

What a shuttle launch costs?
More than half a billion dollars! It also takes the work of 40,000 engineers and space scientists.

How fast humans are launched into space by rocket travel?
They are launched at 7 mi. (11km) a second. As they wait to be launched, they are sitting on the equivalent of a firework 100 ft (30m) high.

What a huge number of parts there are in a rocket or spacecraft?
America's first spacecraft, the Mercury, contained 7 mi. (11km) of electric wire. There were 30,000 parts in a *Saturn 5* rocket.

How for centuries people have dreamed about journeying to the Moon?
Around 165 A.D., the writer Lucian of Samosata wrote the first known space story. His *Vera Historia*, or *True History*, relates the adventures of a shipload of Greek athletes who are blown to the Moon.

How great the atmospheric pressure at the surface of Venus is?
It is 90 times greater than that of Earth. The temperature is so high that lead would melt.

How much fuel the space shuttle uses?
It uses more than 1,500,000 lb. (680,000kg) of liquid oxygen and hydrogen. The shuttle's three engines only work for 8 minutes on each flight. In that time, they use all the fuel—and the shuttle has traveled from Earth into space.

What "planetary science" is?
This branch of astronomy studies the planets and minor bodies of our solar system. It brings together elements of chemistry, physics, geology, and meteorology.

What "cosmology" is?
This branch of astronomy looks at the universe as a whole. It became a proper science during the first half of the 1900s with the building of the first generation of giant telescopes and the general theory of relativity, devised by Albert Einstein (1879–1955). Today, cosmologists wrestle with questions such as exactly how the universe came into being and how it might eventually come to an end.

Which star groupings there are in the universe?
Stars contain most of the visible matter in the universe. These giant balls of hot gas do not float about on their own, but are grouped together in a number of different ways. They spend their infancy in stellar nurseries called open clusters, with up to 10,000 other stars. Open clusters are gradually pulled apart by the gravity of their surroundings. Galaxies do not float freely in space but form clusters of galaxies. The Milky Way is part of a galaxy cluster called the Local Group.

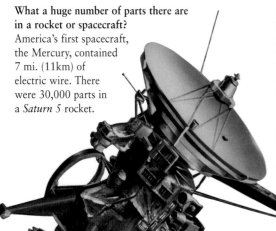

What the word "astrophysics" means?
It means simply "the physics of the stars." This type of astronomy analyzes starlight, which can help explain the structure and evolution of galaxies.

Who the first paying space tourist was?
In 2001, Dennis Tito, an American engineer and multimillionaire, was the first space tourist to pay for his own ticket to travel into space. In that year, he spent 7 days, 22 hours, and 4 minutes in orbit around Earth on *Soyuz TM-32*, the International Space Station, and *Soyuz TM-31*. He paid $20 million dollars for his trip!

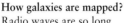

How galaxies are mapped?
Radio waves are so long that they can penetrate the clouds of dust that hide most of our galaxy from view. Free hydrogen atoms in space emit radio waves at a wavelength of 8 in. (21cm). If the atom emitting the radio waves is moving away from us, this will cause the wavelength to appear slightly longer. If the source is approaching us the wavelength will be shorter. Radio astronomers use this to map galaxies.

That Earth is in danger from objects from outer space?
The sky is being monitored for so-called Near-Earth Objects, such as comets or large meteorites, to provide warnings of possible future threats to Earth. Governments could then first nuclear missiles into space to shatter the threat before it entered Earth's atmosphere. However, if a really large meteorite were to head our way, Earth would stand no chance at all.

Which is the most famous comet of all?
In the 1600s, the astronomer Edmond Halley noticed similarities between a comet he had seen in 1607 and one witnessed in 1682. He worked out that it was actually the same comet that passes Earth every 76 years. The last sighting of Halley's comet was 1986. The Bayeux Tapestry, an embroidered artwork commissioned by William the Conqueror of England between 1066 and 1077 depicts its 1066 appearance.

What shape galaxies are?
Edwin Hubble classified galaxies into elliptical, spiral, barred, and irregular types. Almost three-quarters of the galaxies in the universe are elliptical (shaped like an egg). Spiral galaxies have arms emerging from a central bulge—the Milky Way is a spiral galaxy. Barred galaxies are similar in shape but have a central bridge of stars that link the inner ends of the spiral arms. Irregular galaxies are galaxies that do not fit any of these shapes.

Who first saw the Milky Way?
Galileo first observed our galaxy through a telescope and found that it was made of millions of stars. Parts of the Milky Way can easily be seen in the night sky, but most of it is blotted out by dust. Astronomers use radio waves to "see" the whole picture.

What the size of the Sun is?
The Sun is the star that gives heat and light to our solar system. It is a huge, fiery gas ball more that 300,000 times the size of Earth. By converting hydrogen to helium, it makes vast amounts of energy. Without this energy, there would be no life on Earth. There is enough hydrogen to last 5,000 million years.

GLOSSARY

arachnoid A type of volcano with ridges around it that resembles a spider's body and legs when seen from above. First discovered on the planet Venus.

asteroid A lump of rock or metal, usually smaller than a planet and without an atmosphere or moons orbiting it, but larger than a meteoroid. Most asteroids orbit the Sun. They are sometimes called minor planets.

asteroid belt The zone between the outermost inner planet Mars and the innermost outer planet Jupiter, where millions of asteroids orbit the Sun.

astronomer Someone who studies the planets, stars, moons, and other bodies and objects in space.

astronomy The study of planets, stars, moons, and other space bodies, also of space itself and the whole of the universe. Astronomy is partly a practical science that involves observing and cataloging. *see* **cosmology**

atmosphere The layer of gases surrounding a planet or star.

axis An imaginary line passing through the middle of a star or planet, around which the object spins or rotates.

Big Bang An unimaginably gigantic explosion, thought to have happened at the beginning of the universe more than 13 billion years ago, and perhaps when space, time, and matter began.

black hole A very small, dense, dark area of space with immensely powerful gravity, created when a star collapses to less than nothing and pulls in everything around it, including light.

coma A bright glowing cloud, or "halo," around a body such as a comet.

comet A relatively small ball of rock and ice, known as a "dirty snowball," orbiting the Sun on a very lop-sided path that may take it far beyond the distance of Pluto to the Oort cloud.

constellation A pattern or picture seen in a group or cluster of stars as they are viewed from Earth.

core The central part of a planet, moon, star, or other space object.

corona The glowing ring or "halo" around the Sun, best seen during a solar eclipse when the Moon passes in front of the Sun.

cosmology The development of astronomy dealing with the origin and evolution of the universe as a whole and how it works.

crater A bowl- or dish-shaped hollow on a planet, moon, or asteroid, caused by another object crashing into it.

crust The hard rocky outer layer of a planet, such as Earth.

dark matter Invisible material that we cannot detect using scientific methods, but which is thought to make up a large percentage of the universe.

day The amount of time it takes a planet or moon to spin around once on its axis, so that its closest star returns to the same point in its sky.

dwarf star A star that is smaller than the Sun.

eclipse When one space object, such as a moon, goes between another object and a star, as when the Moon moves between the Sun and Earth and casts a shadow on Earth.

equator An imaginary line around the middle of a planet or moon, at right angles to its axis of rotation (spin).

galaxy A huge cluster of stars, planets, and other objects held together in space by gravity, and with immense distances of almost empty space to the next galaxies.

gas giants Jupiter, Saturn, Uranus, and Neptune, the four largest outer planets in the solar system, that are made mostly of gases.

giant star A star that is bigger than the Sun.

gravity A force that makes any object or matter pull or attract other objects toward it. Gravity often refers to Earth's gravity, and gravitational force to the general name of the force that acts everywhere throughout the universe. The gravitational force is one of only four fundamental forces in the universe (the others are electromagnetic force, strong nuclear force, and weak nuclear force).

hemisphere Half of a star, planet, moon, or similar object, usually either above (north) or below (south) of its equator.

inner planets Mercury, Venus, Earth, and Mars, the four smaller and mainly rocky planets of the inner solar system, closest to the Sun.

Kuiper belt A zone of orbiting asteroid- or comet-like objects in the outer solar system, orbiting the Sun beyond Neptune. Its existence was first proposed in 1951 by U.S. astronomer Gerard Kuiper.

lander A spacecraft, or part of one, designed to land on another space object, such as a planet or moon, or to plunge into the atmosphere of a gassy object, such as Jupiter. It can be crewed by astronauts or unmanned and remote-controlled.

lens A curved piece of glass that bends or refracts light, as used in telescopes, binoculars, and microscopes.

lunar Having to do with Earth's moon.

lunar eclipse When Earth passes between the Sun and the Moon, casting a shadow on the Moon.

mantle A layer of rock or other material that lies between the core and the outer surface of a planet or moon.

mass The amount of matter in an object. The numbers and types of atoms or their subatomic particles, independent of any gravity acting on them.

meteor A meteoroid that enters Earth's atmosphere and burns up, appearing as a bright streak of light, also called a shooting star or falling star.

meteorite A meteoroid that falls all the way to Earth's surface.

meteoroid A small chunk of rock, metal, ice, or a mixture of these, usually broken off a comet or an asteroid.

Milky Way Our galaxy that contains the solar system.

moon A space object that orbits a planet.

NASA (National Aeronautics and Space Administration) The government space agency of the U.S.A.

nebula A huge cloud of gas and dust in space, often where new stars are forming. A planetary nebula is a "shroud" of gas thrown off by an overheating or fading star.

neutron star The small, incredibly dense remnant of a star that has exploded and collapsed into a ball of subatomic particles called neutrons.

observatory A building or site where telescopes are used to observe objects in space.

orbit To go around and around another object. The orbit of a planet or moon is its path around another object, such as the Sun. Most orbits are not circular, but elliptical (oval).

orbiter A spacecraft or part of one that orbits its destination, rather than carrying out a flyby or trying to land on the surface.

Oort cloud A huge, ball-shaped cloud of comets and similar objects surrounding the entire solar system.

planet A large, spherical, rocky, and/or gassy object orbiting a star. Planets can be defined and distinguished from other objects, such as asteroids, by their size, whether they orbit around a star or whether they have an atmosphere.

pole The point on a rotating space object where the imaginary line around which it spins, the axis of rotation, passes through its surface.

pulsar A rapidly rotating neutron star that sends out beams of radio and other energy as it spins, like a

lighthouse, and appears to flash or blink on and off.

Radar (Radio Direction And Ranging) A way of measuring shapes and distances of objects by bouncing or reflecting radio waves off them.

satellite Any object that orbits another object in space, whether natural, such as a moon, or artificial, such as a space station. Often used for artificial or man-made objects orbiting Earth, such as communication satellites, comsats, and weather satellites, meteosats.

Sol The scientific name for the Sun.

solar Having to do with the Sun.

solar eclipse When the Moon passes between the Sun and Earth, blocking out the Sun's light.

solar system The Sun and all the planets, moons, and other objects that orbit around it or each other.

spacecraft Any kind of vehicle or vessel built for travel in space. This name is often used for a crewed vehicle, one carrying astronauts.

space probe A small, crewless spacecraft sent to explore space and send information or data back to Earth.

space station A relatively large space base orbiting Earth, where people can stay for long periods.

star A relatively large space object that, for part of its existence, contains nuclear fusion reactions that produce heat and light, making it shine. There are many types of stars, such as white dwarfs, brown stars, and neutron stars.

sunspot A darker, cooler area on the Sun's surface.

supergiant star A very large, bright giant star.

supernova The massive explosion at the end of a supergiant star's life.

telescope A device that makes faraway things seem bigger, used for studying space. Optical telescopes detect light rays, while other types detect other forms of electromagnetic rays or radiation, such as radio waves, infrared, UV (ultraviolet), and X-rays.

transit When one relatively small space object is seen passing across the face of a larger, farther one, such as when Venus passes across the face of the Sun, as seen from Earth.

Trojans Two groups of asteroids following the same orbit around the Sun as Jupiter, one group in front of the planet and the other behind.

universe Everything that has ever existed, is existing, and ever could exist, including all of space and all its contents.

year The amount of time a planet takes to complete one full orbit around its star.

FURTHER READING
& WEBSITES

BOOKS

1001 Facts About Space (Backpack Books)
Sue Grabham (Dorling Kindersley, 2002)

Building Cards: How to Build Spaceships
Doug Stillinger (Klutz, 2006)

More Telescope Power: All New Activities and Projects for Young Astronomers
Gregory L. Matloff (Jossey-Bass, 2002)

Mysteries in Space: A Chapter Book
(True Tales: Exploration and Discovery)
Rosanna Hansen (Children's Press (CT), 2006)

Mysterious Universe: Supernovae, Dark Energy, and Black Holes (Scientists in the Field)
Ellen Jackson (Houghton Mifflin Books for Children, 2008)

Space Exploration (Discovery Channel School Science)
Betsy Rasmussen (Gareth Stevens Publishing, 2003)

Space Exploration (DK Eyewitness Books)
Carole Stott (Dorling Kindersley, 2009)

Space Exploration (How It Works)
Steve Parker (Mason Crest Publishers, 2010)

Space Exploration (Mission: Science)
Connie Jankowski (Compass Point Books, 2008)

Space Exploration (Space Innovations)
Ron Miller (Twenty-First Century Books (CT), 2007)

Space Exploration (Space Travel Guides)
Giles Sparrow (Franklin Watts, 2010)

Space Exploration and Humanity: A Historical Encyclopedia (2 volumes)
American Astonautical Society and Stephen Barry Johnson (ABC-CLIO, 2010)

Space, Stars, and the Beginning of Time:
What the Hubble Telescope Saw
Elaine Scott (Clarion Books, 2010)

The Hubble Space Telescope (True Books-Space)
Diane M. and Paul P. Sipiera (Children's Press, 1998)

The Kingfisher Young People's Book of Space
Martin Redfern (Kingfisher, 1998)

The Story of the Exploration of Space
(Adventures in the Real World)
Penny Clarke (Book House, 2007)

WEBSITES

www.kidsastronomy.com/
A comprehensive site that gives information about planets, asteroids, and comets, as well as other objects in deepest space, and details about space exploration and civilian space travel. Features an astronomy dictionary, games, and sky maps.

www.nasa.gov/audience/forstudents/5-8/index.html
The NASA site that gives the most up-to-date information about missions, planets, and space science, with fantastic photographs, games, and career tips.

www.esa.int/esaKIDSen/index.html
The European Space Agency (ESA) site, with news and information about everything to do with space, from the first flights to the present day, giving analysis of the lastest satellite pictures showing climate change, as well as games and activities.

www.cosmos4kids.com/
Gives great basic information about all kinds of space and astronomical topics, with links to other space and science sites.

www.neok12.com/Space-Exploration.htm
A collection of videos that answer questions and give information about various aspects of space travel, including a tour of the International Space Station; includes downloadable photographs and games.

www.astronomy-for-kids-online.com/
A comprehensive site that explores space through the eyes of an astronomer, including information about famous astronomers, the Big Bang, how telescopes work, and where the astronomical observatories are to be found in the world.

www.space.com/
A round-up of the latest news on space and spacecraft, with videos, articles, and skywatching highlights; also has quizzes and movie reviews.

INDEX

A

Aldrin, Edwin "Buzz" 18
Andromeda nebula 21
animals in space 17, 32
Apollo missions 14, 15, 18–19, 20, 13
Arecibo message 37
Arecibo radio telescope 25, 37
Ariane rocket 14, 22
armillary spheres 7
Armstrong, Neil 18, 25
asteroids 25, 36, 38
astronauts 19, 20–21, 26, 27, 31, 32, 33, 38, 39
astronomers 4, 6, 7, 8–9, 10, 12–13, 24, 28, 29, 31, 37, 41
Atlantis space shuttle 32, 33
atmosphere 13, 16, 29, 30

B

Big Bang 28, 40–41
black holes 34–35

C

calendars 5, 6
Cassini/Huygens probe 24, 29
Challenger space shuttle 24, 26
COBE (Cosmic Background Explorer) 28
Collins, Michael 18
comets 11, 29, 38
constellations 5, 8–9, 31, 37
Copernicus, Nicolaus 6, 7, 11

D

Delta Clipper 38
Discovery space shuttle 23

E

Earth 4, 5, 6, 7, 8, 9, 10, 11, 12, 13, 14, 15, 16, 18, 20, 21, 22, 24, 25, 26, 29, 36, 38, 41
Einstein, Albert 34
electromagnetic spectrum 12
Endeavour space shuttle 31
ESA (European Space Agency) 14, 22, 23, 24, 29, 30, 33
"event horizon" 34
Explorer 16, 21

F

flotation collars 19
food 20

G

Gagarin, Yuri 21
galaxies 4, 12, 15, 30, 31, 36, 40–41
Galilei, Galileo 4, 5, 12
Galileo probe 29
geocentric theory 6, 7
Giotto probe 14, 22, 25
Glenn, John 20, 21
Goddard, Robert 14, 17
gravitation 11, 15, 25

H

HII rocket 15
Halley's comet 22, 25
heliocentric theory 6, 7
Herschel, Caroline 11
Herschel, Sir William 10, 11
Hubble, Edwin 21, 24, 40
Hubble Space Telescope 13, 29, 30–31

I

infrared 16

J

Jansky, Karl 21
Japan, space programme 15, 22, 24
Jupiter 10, 24, 25, 36, 37

K

Kuiper Belt 24

L

Laika 17
light years 4
Luna probes 18, 19

M

Magellan probe 11
MMU (Manned Maneuvering Unit) 21
Mariner probes 22, 23, 24
Mars 24, 25, 29, 38
Mars Pathfinder probe 25, 29
Mercury 23
Mercury spacecraft 21
META (Megachannel Extra Terrestrial Array) 37
meteorites 4, 16
microwave radiation 17, 28, 36
Milky Way Galaxy 4, 8–9, 10, 12, 21
Mir space station 25, 26, 29, 32, 33, 39
Moon 5, 6, 7, 10, 14, 15, 18, 19, 22, 25, 38
moons 24, 25

N

NASA (National Aeronautics and Space Administration) 16, 23, 24, 25, 26, 30, 36, 38
NASDA (National Space Development Agency) 15
nebulae 4, 8–9, 10, 11, 35
Neptune 11, 24, 25, 29, 37
neutron stars 34–35
Newton, Sir Isaac 11

O

observatories 4, 10, 28, 29

P

Pioneer plaque 36
Pioneer probe 24, 25, 36
planets 4, 5, 6, 7, 22, 23, 24–25, 36
Pluto 21, 24, 39
probes 12, 14, 19, 22–23, 24–25, 27
propellants 14
Ptolemy (Claudius Ptolemaeus) 5, 6
pulsars 28, 34

Q

quasars 28

R

radiation 16, 28
radio astronomy 12, 36
Remote Manipulator Arm 31
Ride, Sally 27
rings, planetary 24, 25
rockets 5, 14–15, 19, 26, 27, 38
Royal Observatory, Greenwich 10, 11

S

satellites 5, 16–17, 27, 28, 30, 33, 38
Saturn 10, 24, 25, 29, 36, 37
Saturn V rocket 15
SETI (Search for Extra Terrestrial Intelligence) 36–37
Shepard, Alan 19, 21, 25
Skylab space station 32, 38
SOHO (Solar Heliospheric Observatory) 29
Sojourner 25, 29
solar atmosphere 29
solar panels 30, 31, 32
solar systems 4, 5, 12, 22, 24, 29, 30, 36, 38
solar winds 23

Soyuz spacecraft 21
spacecraft 5, 15, 20, 21, 22, 33
space hotels 39
Spacelab space station 33
space shuttles 20, 25, 26–27, 29, 33, 38, 39
space stations 26, 32–33, 38, 39
spectrum 12
Sputnik satellites 16, 17, 21
stars 4, 5, 6, 8–9, 12, 13, 21, 28, 30, 31, 34–35, 36, 38
Sun 5, 6, 7, 10, 22–23, 24, 28, 29, 35
supernovae 34–35

T

telescopes 10–11, 12, 13, 28–29, 30, 37
telescope, radio 12, 28, 36, 37
telescopes, reflecting 10–11, 13, 30
telescopes, refracting 10–11, 13
Telstar 17, 25
Tereshkova, Valentina 20
time travel 34, 35
Titan 12, 29
Tombaugh, Clyde 21
Tsiolkovsky, Konstantin 14, 15, 17

U

ultraviolet 16, 29, 30
Ulysses probe 23
Upper Atmosphere Research Satellite 16
Uranus 10, 24, 37

V

Van Allen belt 16
Venera probes 22
Venus 22
Verne, Jules 14, 17
Very Large Array telescope 25, 16
von Braun, Wernher 14
Vostock spacecraft 20, 21
Voyager probes 24, 25, 29, 37

W

weightlessness 20, 33
white dwarfs 35
wormholes 35

X

X-rays 16, 28, 34

ACKNOWLEDGMENTS

The publisher would like to thank: Graham Rich and Hazel Poole for their assistance. Picture research by Image Select.

Picture Credits: t=top, b=bottom, c=center, l=left, r=right, OFC=outside front cover
Ann Ronan: 10cl. Ann Ronan @ Image Select: 4cl, 5br, 6tl, 7br, 7tr, 4/5t, 5cl, 14ct, 14cr, 19tl, 21ct. Art Archive: 41b. Bridgemann Art Library: 4cb, 4/5cb, 6bl, 7tl, 10/11b, 10tl, 11br. British Museum: 7c. Fratelli Alinari: 10b. Images: 37bl. Image Select; 4/5c, 11cr. Kobal Collection; 25t, 36/37c, 38tl. National Maritime Museum; 6/7c. NASA; 21br, 25tr, 39t. NASA/Roger Ressmeyer/Corbis: OFC. Novosti (London): 16bl, 17bl. Planet Earth Pictures: 14l, 14/15b, 15tr, 16tl, 17ct, 18cl, 19br, 20/21b, 22tl, 22/23c, 23cb, 23ct, 24/25c, 25c, 25bl, 26cl, 26bl, 26tl, 27tr, 28/29c, 29cr, 31t, 32tl, 233bl, 32/33b, 36tl. Rex Features: 20tl, 32bl. Science Photo Library: 18bl, 18/19b, (George Baird/US Army) 38/39b, (John Bova) 29cb, (Julian Baum) 22bl, 22/23(main pic), (John Fassanito/NASA) 32/33t, (Bruce Frisch) 39cb, (Philippe Gontier/Eurelios) 28tl, (Hale Observatories) 30/31b, (Galia Jerrican) 28bl, (NASA) 14/15b, 16cb, 17br, 18tr, 20br, 33tr, 37c, 38cb, (Novosti) 14cb, 16/17c, 18/19b, (David Parker) 36bl, 37tr, (Space Telescope Science Institute/NASA) 19bl, 19br, (Deltev van Ravenswaay) 29t. Shimizu Corporation; 39br. Telegraph Colour Library; 4tl, 5ct, 18cr, 18tl, 20/21t & 26c, 24tl, 25t, 26/27c, 27br, 27c, 30tl, 30bl

NOTE TO READERS
The website addresses are correct at the time of publishing. However, due to the ever-changing nature of the Internet, websites and content may change. Some websites can contain links that are unsuitable for children. The publisher is not responsible for changes in content or website addresses. We advise that Internet searches should be supervised by an adult.